The Devil's Dictionary of Corporate Lingo:

From Corporate Angel to Corporate Zombie

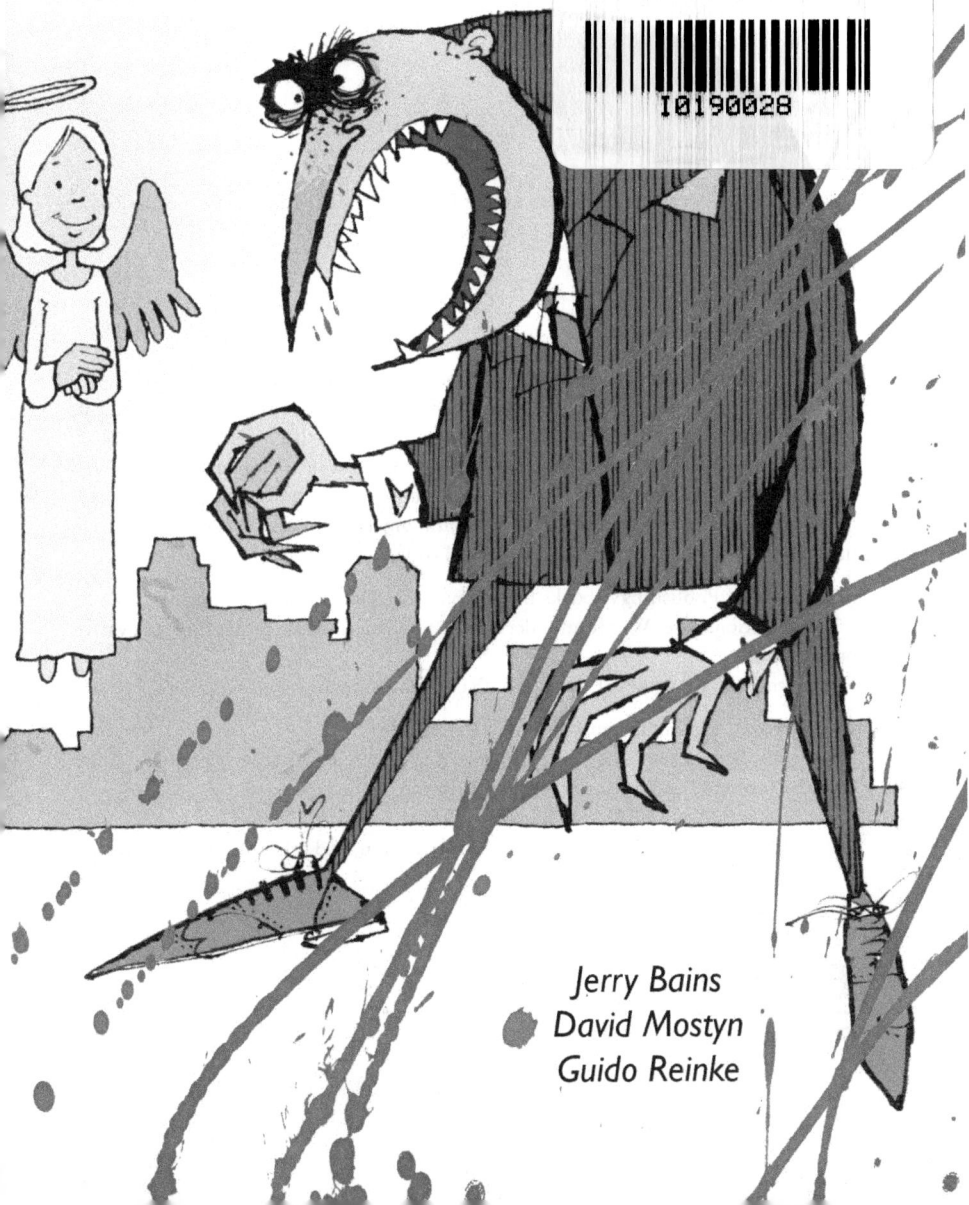

Jerry Bains
David Mostyn
Guido Reinke

**GOLD
RUSH
Publishing**

Readers of this book are cordially invited to submit not only your comments but also concepts of corporate denizens, zookeepers or characters that you have known and believe ought to be included in this *Dictionary*. Concepts for accompanying cartoons are also most welcome.

Please direct all communications to info@GoldRushPublishing.org.

By submitting such items, you agree to relinquish all copyrights to Gold Rush Publishing, and agree that the items may be published in subsequent editions of this book entitled The Devil's Dictionary of Corporate Lingo or under any other title. All contributors who include their names will be acknowledged.

The authors

Table of Contents

Table of Illustrations

For Whom The Devil Wrote This Dictionary

The following dictionary of definitions is the Devil's own guide to digesting human souls inside the belly of that Moloch which is the corporation in today's world. It presents the lingo of corporate-speak, and in doing so it exhibits how *corporate insiders* do the Devil's work. Many people have figured out that corporations live by consuming their customers; only corporate employees understand that the consumption begins on the inside.

In referring to the "corporation", this dictionary does not mean small or medium-sized companies, but multi-nationals which contain the entire human zoo and its keepers. As Gordon Gekko said in the classic movie *Wall Street*: "Greed is Good – Now it seems it's legal – it's about the game – everybody's drinking the same Kool-Aid". Dutifully everybody follows the senior management Pied Pipers, just as 900 followers were led to their deaths by cult-leader Jim Jones, who made them drink from the same poisoned cup. When boards of directors play with *corporate dynamite* through hostile takeovers that are doomed to fail betraying stakeholders and investors alike, big bonuses are their pay-out, while the *small fry* helplessly watch as their careers are made "redundant" and their retirement pensions zeroed out.

Employees on the inside talk to each other about these things over corporate catch-up coffee, but they must never leave any "paper trail" of their innermost feelings. This is where the Devil's Dictionary of Corporate Lingo comes in – to document lexicographically "what oft was thought but ne'er so well expressed" (A. Pope). Best of all is that NO regulator, NO management board, NO chief executive, NO legal counsel or ethics committee approved this dictionary. The Devil's Dictionary records the essence of what so many employees think, but never dared express. There are many business dictionaries out there, but this is the only dictionary of corporate lingo in print that has the Devil's "blessing".

The authors of this work are *corporate renegades* who, like Jonah three days in the whale, have survived at least that long (alas! much longer) inside the belly of the beast. For those who prefer images to lingo, some of the latter have been transmuted into cartoons, which seems appropriate for looking down on the corporate world from a Mephisphelean viewpoint as an endless comic strip. If life imitates art, then the *Devil's Dictionary of Corporate Lingo* is a *corporate special event* captured in print, which consists of *Revelation* in every sense.

This dictionary is dedicated to all employees who have ever vegetated in 3x5-foot *corporate cubicle farms*. It is dedicated to those who, like the homeless, are still living out of their suitcases, working double-time for so long they qualify for every frequent-flyer Platinum card out there. It is dedicated to every living soul who ever felt the *corporate blues* or survived serial *corporate mental abuse*. It is written for the *corporate mushroom* who was stepped on once too often and feels like releasing its toxin. It is written for the *corporate small fry* who have had enough of being treated like plankton in the ocean. It is written in honour of the *corporate A-Team* who never baulked at going the *corporate extra mile*, and of the *corporate heroes* who at least tried to save the day. But it is also written to do fitting homage to the *corporate fatcats* who skim the big bonuses and pay rises, and the way they leave enough of the protein-rich peanuts to *corporate fried anchovies*. It is for the *corporate cowboys* in their high

Introduction

saddles who stand above corporate law, and for the *corporate celebrity* who walks on the red carpet and is an inspiration to the rest of us. And who can forget the *corporate surfer* updating his LinkedIn account and Twittering his stable of headhunters by smart phone of his readiness to surf to the next corporate shore? Above all this Dictionary is dedicated to our *corporate buddies* and our *corporate gurus*, who by some miracle have conserved their ethical compass in working order, and to whom we instinctively turn for clues that may lead us the way out of the *corporate labyrinth*.

Gordon Gekko summed up the corporation a long time ago, "It's all about bucks, kid. The rest is conversation." But conversation may nonetheless entertain, as the following Dictionary will show.

Corporation: The law defines a corporation as a single person existing in legal Never-Never Land, an "entity" completely separate from its real being: teeming multitudes of living, suffering human beings. A corporation is neither real nor fantastical, but merely "unreal" – rather like a zombie is "undead". "Legal personhood" gives the corporation unique powers which real human beings can only envy, for example limited liability means the corporation can avoid paying for losses that are "peanuts" to itself but to the loser may be his life savings. In principle, corporations are immortal: they can exist for hundreds of years if not swallowed up by take-overs, mergers or acquisitions, or succumbed to unsustainable cash flow or unprofitability. Modern corporations are the living embodiments of the doctrine of Social Darwinism, according to which only the fittest *deserve* to survive.

- A -

Corporate Angel: Not every office has one, but you can feel the difference in the office that does. It's the friendly receptionist who puts you through to the "Big Cheese" when you're desperately short of time, or the helpful P.A. (Personal *Angel*) who warns you of the bad temper that's making the Big Cheese stink like Limberger today. The modern office angel doesn't always sport wings and a long robe, but she is nonetheless an angel of mercy protecting you from the usual office devilry. But don't stretch her patience to the breaking point – she just might turn into a Hell's Angel!

Corporate Abuse: A catch-all term for business as usual inside the corporate beast, it signifies the reality that those in command of organizations exploit their hierarchical superiority for personal gain. According to legend *corporate abuse* is contrary to the corporation's code of ethics, although veterans insist such a code is pure superstition. *Corporate abuse* may in theory be unlawful – but just try proving it in court and you will find out how

Corporate Angel

fast evidence disappears into the shredder. Serial *corporate abusers* make the most successful of businessmen: the more respectable and debonair they appear, the more voluminous their criminal record.

Corporate Ambush: Your secretarial job spec says nothing about spending 100 hours organizing the Christmas party, but suddenly you get tasked by upper management to run the show. You've been ambushed! *Corporate ambushers* lurk at every corporate meeting, telco and event. Starting out as an annoyance which brings you few if any *corporate brownie points*, the extra work eventually eats up all the time you need to meet your usual responsibilities. What black magic is it that can convert the kindliest family man or the mousiest secretary into fiendish *corporate ambushers?* The answer is as simple as it is profound: *corporate pressure* – the pressure to go the *corporate extra mile* or be branded a troublemaker.

Corporate Appraisal: This is the time for a full and formal assessment of you from the powers that be higher up. It's decision time! There can be no more alibis. It's too late now to think of how you could have done things better or differently. The day of reckoning has come, and that makes your heart skip a beat. Once you walk into the executive office to face a *corporate appraisal,* you find out your real value to the corporation. Welcome to the world of *corporate small fry*!

Corporate A-Team: They are like the four heroes of the American television action series, Special Forces personnel in the US Army become fugitives accused of "a crime they didn't commit". There is a Lieutenant-Colonel John "Hannibal" Smith, a Lieutenant Templeton "Face" Peck, a Captain H. M. "Howling Mad" Murdock and a Sergeant First Class Bosco (Mr. T) in every corporation. They work long hours, deliver outstanding work with measurable results, have the ability to see the big picture, and never baulk at going the *corporate extra mile*. But as in the fictional

Corporate A Team

realm, so in the world of *corporate reality:* the A-Team can expect no rewards (in the form of bonuses, for example) proportional to their true merits. The bosses coolly reap what they did not sow; the *A-Team* merely do the sweaty harvesting.

Corporate Away Day: The corporation's most solemn rite, when it endeavours to achieve its highest objectives of executive training, team building, and what corporations call "human resource development". Sadly for these lofty objectives, the *corporate small fry* are too mind-numbed by their drudge work to be properly mind-controlled … er, made good corporate citizens. Instead, they hijack this event for their own, somewhat different objectives: indulging in *corporate binge drinking*, starting up affairs, and exchanging the latest *corporate gossip.*

- B -

Corporate Bandwidth: Technically the frequency spectrum within which signals can be transmitted *via* a computer network or other telecommunication system. Real bandwidth is limited by resources, technology, capital costs and time. Corporate lingo, however, distinguishes imaginary from real bandwidth. Senior management are prone to imagining all kinds of limitless "bandwidths", the meaning of which has been lost in transmission, when trying to impress. In the bosses' minds, no human limitations exist apart from their own. *Corporate small fry* are franker: asked if they will take on additional work of a Friday afternoon, they simply respond, "I doubt I'll have the bandwidth so late in the week".

Corporate Benchmarking: A form of evidence-gathering "undertaken" by the gravediggers in HR to bemoan how fatally ill you have performed in the past fiscal year. Of course, if done at the organisational level benchmarking is little more than a nuisance, but on the individual level it feels like a dentist's drill without the Novocain.

The possibilities for benchmarking you individually are endless: against your business unit, your whole organisation, nationally, internationally – you can even be benchmarked against your competitors, or the male or female workforce. It's all nonsense, but hey, it keeps the HR drones busy and mercilessly pressurises the *corporate small fry*. Indeed, the life of a *small fry* is all about benchmarking, using the most *labile* standards. *Corporate benchmarking* keeps you skinny, dumb and less unhappy than if you knew *why* you stay *small fry*, while all around your salary is exceeded by what the *corporate fat cats* make in bonuses alone.

Corporate Binge Drinking: The highlight of every *corporate special event*, when The Land of Milk and Honey becomes a reality for corporate employees from all levels. Alcohol flows without limit and the lavishness of the appointments incites the basic instincts of primordial animal behaviour. Like the ancient Roman Saturnalia festival (involving lots of red wine), it abolishes hierarchy for a fleeting moment and puts all *corporate slaves* on an equal or near-equal footing with their equally intoxicated superiors. At its bacchanalian climax, *corporate small fry* speak freely about the shortcomings of their bosses; *corporate Casanovas* dance the tango with *corporate bombshells*; *corporate clowns* balance empty Champagne bottles on their noses before any audience that will look on; *corporate angels* and *corporate birds* hug and kiss their bosses in boozy ecstasy; and not seldom newbies are born exactly nine months later!

Corporate Bird: While an ordinary *bird* is a warm-blooded, egg-laying vertebrate with a body covered in feathers and forelimbs modified into wings, a *corporate bird* is a quite distinct species. *Corporate birds* are female employees, as naturally gifted in appearance as nature's most elegant avians, and prone to nesting near higher-ups. They are considered "flighty" – suffering from charming but, eventually, maddeningly habitual lapses of attention. They attract male attention by giggling, making silly jokes, and by their helpless look that resembles an abandoned *chick*.

Corporate Bird

Corporate Bliss: A feeling of ecstasy resulting from episodes of successful corporate endeavour.   Faust felt that ecstasy at just the moment when Mephistopheles finally snared him.   It arises from anything that excites our all-too-human vanity: garnering yet more *corporate brownie points*; being affectionately fussed over by a colleague of the opposite sex; reading in-house reports that cite-to or praise one's work.   *Corporate slaves* of course are barred from such experiences, but *corporate fat cats* – who doubtless could teach Mephistopheles a few lessons! – trip the heights of *corporate bliss*.

Corporate Blues (a.k.a. Distress):   Without doubt the constant state of *corporate slaves* and *prisoners*; for others *corporate blues* is a bout of bitter dejection discouraging you from continuing to work for your "People First" firm.   Typical symptoms include dreams of leading the boss in chains to the guillotine; nightmares of terrifying inquisitions by Quality Assurance auditors; the tragic loss of *corporate brownie points*; and the wistful conviction that you'll always remain a *corporate fried anchovy*.

Corporate Bluff, Master of: A toxic mixture of telling half-truths about yourself and your objectives, and pretending to have knowledge and expertise in an area you hardly know. You may convince your superiors that you're a subject matter expert, then arrange a *corporate telco* to delegate all tasks actually requiring any expertise to *corporate small fry,* since you have no clue yourself.   The self-obsessed *fat cats* will perceive you as bringing "superb management skills" to the corporation.

Corporate insiders will in moments of candour admit that those who reach the top of the *corporate career ladder* aren't really better performers, just *Masters of corporate bluff*.   Like proficient members of the Jedi Order, *corporate bluffers* are martial artists, but of the conniving intellect: – their light-sabre is a forked tongue, their brazen words a deathblow.

Corporate Bliss

Corporate Distress

Corporate Bombshell: A female employee with (shall we say) *assets* of a different kind. She is always wearing clothing that emphasises her portfolio and a charmingly sweet smile. Whenever she needs a favour and you're the lucky winner, that flattering smile is making your ego an offer it can't refuse. And then you wonder why she is up the *corporate career ladder* so much faster than you!

Corporate Bonding: Top management send us all out on corporate team building events supposed to "bond" us into a stronger team benefitting the organisation as a whole. The slickest team members among us, however, "bond" even more effectively with their colleagues – they *bind* them in chains, once fallen into their *corporate ambushes*.

Corporate Bonuses: Everyone believes they should be cut – except those on the receiving end, of course. Bonuses are earned through unremittingly hard work over a short 12-month period, yet at the end everybody and his parrot is jealous. Why don't these sad sacks just join the corporate world and indulge themselves too? Once you snag your bonus, even if your clients' portfolios shrink by 90% and the country is plunged into recession, you never have to pay any of it back.

Corporate Brownie Points: Tokens of illusory worth that circulate only inside the corporation. The prospect of winning *corporate brownie points* is the factor chiefly motivating employee effort (salary being a fixed baseline only revisable in the long run). Like Mickey Mouse paper money at Disneyland – intrinsically worthless yet imputed with value inside the funny firm ... er, farm – *corporate brownie points* turn employees into kids chasing toys. Examples of *corporate brownie points* include *corporate clammy handshakes*, "here doggy, here's your bone" emails of praise from superiors, corporate-branded bric-a-brac (pens, T-shirts, mugs), and whole big boxes of sugary doughnuts.

Corporate Buddy: Under normal circumstances, your *corporate buddy* is your first point of contact for entry into the corporation's internal network: he will guide you toward building ongoing relationships, explaining "how things are done around here". It can't get more corporate-intimate than having a few drinks with your *corporate buddy*. After the first pint you'll know who is leaving the organisation next before it becomes official; after the second he will let you in on all the internal flings and affairs; and by the third he will tip you off where to find the "fast-track career ladder", which is completely unethical but it's "how things work".

Corporate Bucket: What in the normal world is "a cylindrical vessel" in the corporate universe is a label (maybe a stigma) used to "contain" and thus to categorise staff, clients, business solutions in ways that gingerly tiptoe past the truth. You may find out one day that you have been stuck in the *corporate bucket* of "high performers" (those who have eked out their sales targets for once in their wretched existences), or in with the "rising stars" (those who had better outperform themselves next year or else they will be "made redundant"). You don't want to end up in the *"falling* star" bucket for sure: then you would be all set to "kick the bucket"!

Corporate Buddy

- C -

Corporate California Dreamin': The anthem of all Detroit motor workers, as sung by the *The Mamas and the Papas*, it is likewise the aspiration of corporate drudges the world over: – to find oneself suddenly transported to Silicon Valley, where, instead of poring over reams of figures on the three trillionth printout of the week, one is starting up the next high-tech venture that will make billionaires of its founders. *California Dreamin'* affects employees on all levels but in different ways. *Corporate fat cats* dream of that multi-million-dollar home in Beverly Hills or Malibu, while *small fry* dream of being able to tell their bosses to get lost in their Beverly Hills mansions. As *dreamin'* is the triumph of hope over reality, it may be advisable from time to time to peek in on *corporate California reality*.

Corporate California Reality: Quite unlike *California Dreamin'* for most ordinary folks who have to live there: the routine smog alerts in LA, California's imminent default on its debt, unmanageably rising health care costs, gang warfare in Oakland and

South Central LA, and now California's own real-life Godzilla: the exotic fruit fly that is wreaking havoc on the agricultural industry. Hollywood has produced more than 400 movies depicting the destruction of the City of the Angels by fires, earthquakes, volcanoes, floods, wars, and even a few alien invasions. It might be better to stick with *dreamin'* after all!

Corporate Career Ladder: The venerable old Oxford English Dictionary defines ladder as "a series of ascending stages by which someone or something may progress … [*e.g.*] employees on their way up the career ladder". It is well-known how sleepy Oxford lexicographers can be amid their dreaming spires. *The Devil's Dictionary of Corporate Lingo* is much more contemporary, defining *career ladder* as "a non-tangible tool that employees hang onto for dear life, lest they fall and break their necks". Scientifically, prediction of how far up an employee will actually *climb* this ladder may be determined by an equation consisting of three classes of coefficients in rising order of importance.

First and least important are qualifications (Q): real, measurable skills (S) and solid work experience (E) – admittedly needed, but only for getting near enough to the ladder to grasp it. Second and more important are "soft fudge" factors such as fake humility (H), and the ability to bend the truth convincingly and attract attention at *corporate special events*, delicately known as "delegation skills" (D) or sometimes *management* skills. These will get you up past the first rung. Third and far more important still is that indefinable gift for conjuring up "outputs" that justify your presence in the upper reaches of the corporate space, meaning sheer *corporate bluff* (CB) plus frequent attendance of Very Important meetings (M), in which fast-trackers jockey for "position" but anyone else could see nothing happening.

To climb over the top, leaving the ladder behind as no longer needed to cling to, requires something special if not indeed

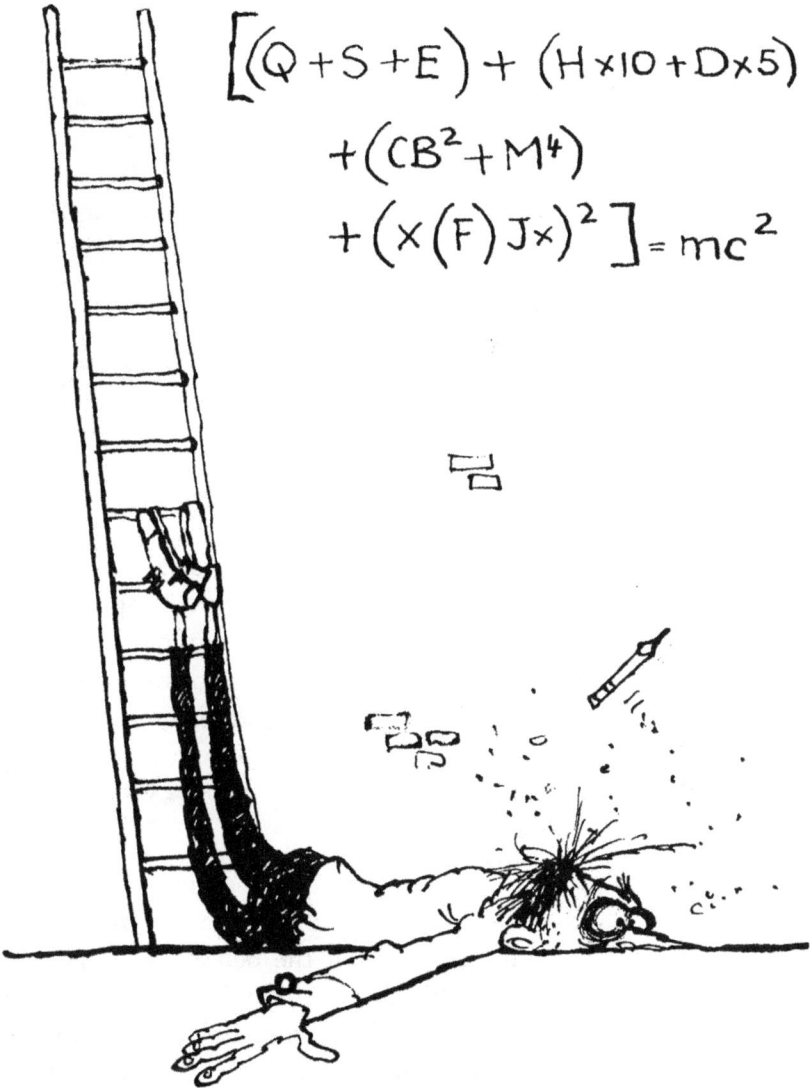

$$\left[(Q+S+E) + (H \times 10 + D \times 5) + (CB^2 + M^4) + (\times(F)J\times)^2\right] = mc^2$$

Corporate Career Ladder

mysterious: just the right X-Factors ($X(F)$) times *mojo*, also known as The Juice (J). And then, it depends on the energy needed to climb (defined as mc^2 by Einstein). To appreciate what it all means requires that you first have a beer or two (or three or four) with your *corporate buddy*. He will calculate it for you according to the following formula, which synthesises all factors into a combinatorial eigen-variable equation of non-linear dynamical phase-space, which topologically defines the phase-transition of vector-autoregressive career-enhancing functions as associated differentiable fractals:

Career ladder ascension $= [(Q + S + E) + (H*10 + D*5) + (CB^2 + M^4) + (X(F)e^{J^1})^{10}]*mc^2$.

Can you remember that tomorrow?

Corporate Casanova: The male counterpart to the *corporate bombshell*. His arts of seducing, admired by male and female colleagues alike, reach their climax at *corporate special events*. To spot him at the office doing actual everyday work is more difficult. But who doesn't remember the muscular colleague who used to go for a jog at lunch time and return to the office in his sporting duds? Or maybe all you remember is the tear-stained face of your attractive secretary – *this* is the "work" of a *corporate Casanova*, for sure.

Corporate Catch-up: *"Unproductive"* catch-ups feature high volumes of *corporate curiosity* and loads of sandwiches and *coffee*. Often they lead to *corporate abuse* through the delegation of all real work to the junior staff. *"Productive"* catch-ups (often corporate workshops, where the bosses look in from time to time, so that everyone is on his best behaviour) result in clearly defined deliverables, decisions and action plans. Senior staff find productive *catch-ups* more agonising than passing a kidney stone: actual hands-on work with laptops and pens, decisions that lay heads on chopping blocks, commitment to real corporate action.

CORPORATE CASANOVA

Corporate Catch-up Coffee: One of those definitive social conventions, the significance of which only the natives fully grasp. As you change people and departments, however, the wink-wink meaning of this social lap-dance grinds and slip-slides all over the place. If offered by someone more senior, this is Morse code for "we need to have a serious heart-to-heart talk about how little work you have been doing". If offered by a *corporate buddy*, it's a secret handshake for "I gotta tell you the latest juicy gossip". But beware: if your *corporate mentor* invites you for *catch-up coffee*, it's a ha-ha sign meaning "The situation is desperate, your ambitions have been stiffed and your career looks totally stuffed".

Corporate Celebrity: What would life be without celebrities? They gossip relentlessly, dress provocatively, and constantly call attention to themselves like movie stars on the red carpet, inspiring envy and emulation in the rest of us. Corporate celebrities are no different. Think of your flashiest, most outspoken colleague. For all his glibness you may not even know what project or division he is working in. What matters to him is that you know *him*. He will be remembered for singing karaoke like a pro at the Christmas Party, or she for her gourmet "poshcakes" at the charity event. Like media celebrities, the *corporate celebrity* is celebrated most of all for being celebrated. Occasionally, one of them will achieve extraordinarily high status, causing the rapid growth of ambient myths alleging superhuman escapades. This may lead on to the cult status of *corporate hero*.

Corporate Clammy Handshake: Senior management get big bonuses, *small fry* get *clammy handshakes* of thanks from their superiors. Some poor souls are rumoured to have postponed washing their hands for weeks after the CEO gave them a sweaty limp-wrister at the Christmas party. "Virtual" *clammy handshakes* are more prestigious (and less infectious). They are distributed in the form of email, telephone messages or honourable mention on the

Corporate Clammy Handshake

TV plasma screen in the lobby. If you should ever see your name up there, you might just do better to blush for shame than swell with pride: it can only mean that your bonus (if any) is too microscopical to be scandalous. By contrast, publicising the details of those receiving the mega-bonuses would be a *shocking* violation of Business Ethics and the human right to Privacy! Your fifteen minutes of fame are already up: a booby prize is still a booby prize, even in our digital age.

Corporate Clown: The one with the big grin and the loud mouth, often spotted with a goofy Santa Claus or Charlie Brown necktie at Christmas parties. He is that rarest of individuals who can find humour in his colleagues' agonistic *movements* deep inside the *bowels* of the corporation. The *corporate cl*own is always sharing his *intestine* jokes and his enlivening *ruminations* with his sadder colleagues. He is fearless in expressing his opinions, believing every corporate *excretion* he becomes *privy* to ought to be *digested* with a *soupçon* of wit and a zest of verve. Through his *lax* behaviour he brings a creeping sense of *relief* and sometimes even *corporate bliss* to the *sluggish* proceedings of many, shall we say, *anal-retentive* personalities. At all events, what a *corporate clown* says is at least *food* for thought.

Corporate Communications: Have you ever wondered why large corporations charge more than small business? It's all to subsidise their internal Communication Departments, who spend a king's ransom (poor souls) cranking out excruciatingly tedious internal newsletters that no one would ever want to read.

Corporate Competitor: These are blood-feud enemies: they are out to cut your throat and skate on your blood (and you theirs), while both of you present sunny little Happy Faces to the public! The two of you will do everything in your power to steal each other's market share, seduce each other's loyal customer base, and headhunt each other's staff more fiercely than cannibals. As in the movie *War of the Worlds, corporate competitors* turn up like a flash of lightning where you least expect it, and fight the kind of war which leaves only one survivor standing.

Corporate Clown

Corporate Competitor

Corporate Complaint: The sheer number of *complaints* with their attached complainers amount to what is called *legion* in the context of demon possession, and a myriad of myriads in the Apocalypse. To try and narrow things down a wee bit, and after analysing the records of more than 300,000 calls from one corporate complaint centre – outsourced in Bangalore, India of course, – Mohit Gandhara informs us: "People in Western countree complain about all things of companee but mostly complains about unfairness in workplace. They are very unhappee, and here in call centre we hear terrible thing, it should make us unhappee too. Luckee thing is, rising call volume from all the unhappee people give big Rupee to us".

Corporate Consultant: If you are an employee who has to hire consultants, these will be the ones you really hate: they get paid twice as much as you for doing half the work. Usually they're a nuisance and a distraction, like cockroaches in the bathroom. You've heard it said before: you ask consultants for the time, they take your watch and read the time back to you without returning it.

Corporate Cowboy: Whilst in British English *cowboy* means a person who is dishonest or careless in business, in American English it connotes a "real man", who spends most of his day on horseback herding and tending cattle. Naturally, management preen themselves on the American way: from their "high saddles" *corporate cowboys* ride herd on their underlings, but their management skills are so *elemental* that the human cattle are prone to stampede in the opposite direction. The Sales Department seems to be their favourite watering-hole.

Corporate Credentials: The sheepskins and bits of tinselled paper that "prove" you aren't as stupid as you look. How odd that so many employees are so fond of these scraps, hanging them all over the walls of their homes and offices. Even one's hairdresser mounts the diploma from his shampoo supplier's training course. The more – the merrier!

Corporate Cowboy

Corporate Cross-Self-Fertilization: Thomas Jefferson once said: "The tree of liberty must be refreshed from time to time with the blood of patriots and tyrants; it is its natural manure". In not quite the same *vein*, the *blood* of the *family* tree is the natural *manure* that from time to time will be found refreshing many (all too many) a corporation. The risk in the long run is getting so cross-self-fertilised as to become downright *inbred*. Typical instances are to be found in the recruitment process. The apprehensive candidate's ears prick up when he hears the interviewer intone, while stifling a yawn, "There are only a few requirements for this job".   The interviewer proceeds, "Are you the boss's wife's cousin's grandson?", to which the interviewee nervously replies, "Unfortunately I am not". The interviewer tries again, "Well then, are you the boss's brother's mistress's illegitimate son?"; the crestfallen response follows, "Unhappily, no". The interviewer however knows when to persist, "… or for that matter, the boss's auntie's stepson?" Brightening up the interviewee says perkily, "Yes; how did you know?" The interview is abruptly terminated: "You're hired".

Corporate Cubical: The modern office is a soulless "cubicle farm" – a rat-maze of identical "mini-offices" designed to treat all workers equally by making them all equally uncomfortable. The inevitable complaints are registered by help desks outsourced in remote countries, and filed under staff numbers associated with a call-reference number for impersonal efficiency. Attempts have allegedly been made to design The *Human* Cubical, supposedly allowing privacy, personalisation and adequate room, but the fact is that the next step in the evolution of the *small fry* warren has been taken: The Open-Space Office – a corporate circus tent where personality and privacy are not even considered, because everybody can see, hear and (above all) smell everything, including the bacon butty of that colleague sitting next to you.

Corporate Curiosity: Although firmly convinced along with John D. Rockefeller that "what the public doesn't know won't hurt them", *corporate insiders* aren't nearly so sanguine about their own unknowing *vis-à-vis* their underlings. *Corporate curiosity*, always initiated from the top down by senior staff, is not a scientist's curiosity in universal truth nor the idle curiosity of boredom, but more like a cat's curiosity in mouse holes. In other words, it is the nature of *corporate curiosity* to *smell blood*.

Corporate Cyberspace: The virtual reality where *corporate geeks* and *freaks* meet to exchange ideas. They fancy themselves somewhere in the clouds, far above it all, where they exchange rude messages about their superiors and the corporation in total privacy. Management wish they could track them down, but their aliases – like "managementsucks" or "wheresmybonus" – are impossible to decode.

- D -

Corporate Daydreamer: The one who looks like he must get paid for contemplating the sky all day long. How he gets his work done will never be known; we all see him gazing out of the window most of the time. But he's still around, so something obviously inspires him, and in turn his attitude in some strange way inspires the rest of us. Something exists outside these corporate walls that makes your heart beat faster. Is it the freedom we had almost forgotten?

Corporate Deadlines: If you don't meet them, this does not mean you will be sacked. It just means that you *will* meet that deadline, or else you're in line to be dead! Without deadlines, clients couldn't be billed nor annual *corporate bonuses* paid on time. On the other hand, if you're in senior management, just *delegate* the damned deadlines! Let mortals fiddle with Microsoft Project and Excel. You're far too busy counting the money.

Corporate Deliverables: It sounds like it might be pizza, except that corporate deliverables contain far more junk and even less real nutrition. Like the pizza boy, corporate employees and consultants deliver something; but unlike his deliverables, theirs can cause line-managers more pain in their stomach linings than a pizza with poisoned mushrooms. A report, a work paper, a mere clutch of completed forms even, may be considered "deliverables" in the white collar world, just so long as they are reviewed, signed off, "processed", and dust-binned (in corporate terms archived). Also unlike pizza boys, who get more tips the more pizzas they deliver, senior management get fatter bonuses the more poisoned mushrooms they pick off – *lest* they be delivered. Thus, in the corporate world the less you actually deliver, the bigger your bonus.

Corporate Downsizing: Similar to *corporate restructuring*, but with yet more shrinkage and redundancies. It means the bosses have so badly mismanaged the department where you worked, that your soul-withering, health-ruining 70 hours a week have come to nought. The Board save their own skin by shutting your department down or selling it off, then awarding themselves bonuses for "turning around an unprofitable firm". Meanwhile, *small fry* get the sack. The "lucky" ones get rehired by corporate outsourcing providers, who redeploy staff at much higher rates to the downsized corporation – leaving the *fat cats* with even bigger bucks. The *small fry*, meanwhile, can eat plankton.

Corporate Dragoman (a.k.a. Interpreter): This is the person in your corporation who knows all the latest buzz words that make consultants tick over and purr. He could translate all that gobbledygook into intelligible terms, but thinks it cool to belong to that distinguished species whose jargon is as encrypted as their data. Once the *corporate dragoman* has adopted a new word he will drive it into the ground in the effort to impress: *"At our next blue sky meeting, we shouldn't boil the ocean, just bounce cutting-edge ideas off the business-development team that will get everyone on the same page* *to create quick win-wins, batch chargeable deliverables, and empower the team to achieve their full potential"*. Translator!

Corporate Drama: The principle advice for survival in the corporate world is, always expect the unexpected. Sometimes even this maxim gets maxed-out, and then you're facing a *corporate drama*. You weren't expecting flowers for your birthday, but a redundancy notice in the post is the last thing you would expect. Or, your department was right on track to meet the year's sales targets, but then one fine day your team leader doesn't turn up for work. You never expected that this dynamic, sun-tanned, debonair all-rounder loved by all *corporate birds* would suffer a heart attack from *corporate pressure* and upend all of the team's expectations.

Corporate Dreaming: Dreaming is a mental event associated with the "rapid-eye-movement" (REM) phase of sleep. Such is their wonderland "logic" that some dreams aren't even thinkable in the sober light of every day. *Corporate dreaming* is like that, except it occurs to employees fully awake during office hours. Examples include "getting considered" – (just considered!) – "for a promotion with salary increase", "a month-long crash of the corporate email server", "booking on an assignment to a client with just half the patience of the Pope", "once in a blue moon attending corporate events in the Caribbean", or "immediate replacement of the canteen cook by someone who can cook". Dream on!!

Corporate Dynamite: Like the subaltern trader whose derivatives dealing caused an entire international investment bank, the ancient and distinguished House of Barings, to implode into a black hole, *corporate dynamite* is the stuff that can turn a solid corporation with a health balance sheet and robust client base into nanometer dust. This could equally be caused by internal fraud, corruption or bribery, financial misconduct or abuse of technology. Clearly, it's something that, if let out of its genie bottle, might set in train a disaster even the *small fry* wouldn't relish witnessing. So long as the fuse hasn't been lit, no harm is done; yet every corporation harbours its own corporate dynamite deep down its crypt. Timely action must be taken, or else one fine day out of the clear blue the corporation may be discovered to be a pile of smoking rubble, worthless for stakeholders and investors alike.

- E -

Corporate Early Bird: Not to be confused with *corporate bird*. A *corporate early bird* is an employee obliged to rise at inhumanely early hours to meet his or her objectives, always under *corporate pressure*. Reasons for the pitiful cawing of these birds may be: client meetings in remote places at ungodly hours, timetabled by superiors in their pyjamas who will join in *via* telco from their hotel suites, or flights booked for the crack of dawn by support staff and secretaries angling to impress the boss with their budget savings. Some *corporate early birds*, however, may just want to be first in the office in order to exchange the latest gossip with an early birdsong.

Corporate Eggsucker: That most conniving member of the team, who without a hint of warning may have already stolen ideas, deliverables, even whole initiatives and programmes from you and other "team players"; preferably while your ideas are still in their infancy and of uncertain parentage. Having sucked out the eggs others have laid, they "lay" claim to the initiatives or

Corporate Eggsucker

inventions as their own in order to gobble up all the credit and rewards. Those with *fertile* imaginations should avoid close contact: they are a truly dangerous species in the corporate jungle.

Corporate Entertainment: Anything you can do as an amusing distraction from business – so long as it lowers the client's guard. It's routine nowadays to seduce, butter up, mesmerise, massage the ego of, and generally soften up business clients for that deal-closing, velvet hammer sucker-punch. Techniques span the gamut from inviting them for proper English tea at the Ritz, to taking them off to frolic in the sands of the Riviera, – all on the corporate expense account, of course. *Corporate entertainment* is a cat-and-mouse game, except that who the cat is and who the mouse, is not visible on the surface of things. Just keep smiling like the Cheshire Cat as you are whisked away to the evening's *corporate entertainment*.

Corporate Entity: Originating in 16th-century Spain as the Anonymous Society (S.A. or *Sociedad Anónimo*), corporations have always tried to be as faceless to the public, as blankly non-descript as humanly possible. Over the years corporations have learned to avoid labels as frank as "corporation" – (even Anonymous Society is too informative) – preferring the most vacuous label human language can afford. One like "entity". It reflects the Prime Directive and ethical lodestar of all *corporate insiders*: "What the public doesn't know won't hurt them".

Corporate Extra Mile: Think hard if your line-managers ask you to "go the extra mile". Think very hard. Who wouldn't go the extra mile if it made things happen and got you ahead? But what it really means is: working longer hours; doing someone else's work; risking your health to travel at ungodly hours to far destinations. The catch is, senior management will get big bonuses from your going the *extra mile*, while *small fry* normally get little more than a *corporate clammy handshake*. So think twice about every inch next time you're asked to go that extra mile.

CORPORATE ENTERTAINMENT

- F -

Corporate Fatcats: You guessed it: these are the big shots who get all the cream – the big bonuses and pay rises! And they justify their existence by spending more money than you make in several years to ballyhoo to the world how much they are worth it. Always keep them stocked up with the *creme de la creme* and rolling in catnip and clover, or they will scratch you blind. Animal instinct will never change.

Corporate Fate: In the long run we are all dead, as that dismal economist Keynes infamously said. But some of us die in greater agony than others, and in any case our children carry on after us. Could this *Devil's Dictionary* be the most accurate guide yet as to which ultimate fates await which people in today's "People First" corporation? If only we could steer our children away from our own *corporate fate* and toward better chances ...

Corporate Fat Cat

Corporate Feedback: One of many factors impacting how slow ... er, how fast one will climb the *corporate career ladder*. If you want good *corporate feedback*, you'll have to give up on a social or a home life; work interminable hours day in and day out; be stuck away in fluorescent-lit, eye-itchingly air-conditioned project rooms with the same old same old project-mates, until you can recognise them by their smell as much as by their voice; and always remember to shred every document that might embarrass the firm (no end to those!).

Poor *feedback* can be expected if you shirk any of the foregoing; storm out of the project room when you can't take it any more, or slow down your department's LAN by cyber-networking with your friends on the blessed Outside *via* your heavily trafficked Facebook site. Had Thomas Jefferson been a management guru, he could have coined just the right tongue-twisting word-to-the-wise for today's *corporate small fry*: "That *corporate feedback* feeds back best which feeds back *least*".

Corporate Fool: An employee who acts unprofessionally, and is quite properly regarded as unacceptable according to the High Standards and most ethical Values of the corporate entity. Foolish behaviour may range from unwittingly insulting colleagues to volubly defying senior management. *Corporate fools* practically invite management to give them the sack. Their utter guilelessness is their undoing. Some souls just don't have it in them to scheme and plan their every move. These types amuse their colleagues with dopey performances that can be gossiped about endlessly.

Corporate Freak: An employee whose obsessiveness or eccentricity can instigate the oddest behaviour. *Corporate freaks* can often be detected by their addiction to work: horny calluses on their fingers from excessive typing on keyboards, dashing down corridors late for the next meeting, or their boasting, without too much exaggeration, that they have been working 24/7. Do they live to work or work to live?

Corporate Fried Anchovy (a.k.a. Graduate Trainee): Slightly bigger than *corporate small fry* and in their own (but only their *own*) belief more important, the *corporate fried anchovy* is what management have for breakfast. The well-groomed, Oxbridge-educated new joiner in a designer suit may grab the ladies' attention when he strides into the office and introduces himself to all. He may vapour-on as much as he likes of how valuable he would be and what a difference he would make to the corporation. Once hired, then he finds out from the boss's secretary where his new office will be: "See that cubby hole next to the janitor's room?" The *corporarte fried anchovy* sighs, puzzling over his fate: "Even the janitor has a proper office, but not a VIP like me?!"

- G -

Corporate Geek: This is the poor devil whose shyness and entertaining social dysfunctionality his colleagues are all whispering about. He doesn't actually bite heads off chickens, but you wouldn't know it listening to the gossip. He's the same chap who couldn't hold his liquor at the last *corporate special event* and, losing his inhibitions under its influence, made a fool of himself. At least the blessed soul is too far out of the social loop to hear the gossip himself ... usually.

Corporate Gordon Gekko: A loner whom no one ever notices. He is always punctual for work and always does what he is told. He has no time for socialising, never takes risks, and never slips up at his work. He's like the proverbial slow-walking fly-on-the-wall, except much smarter and very target-oriented. He leaves the company as unnoticed as he came. Before you know it a start-up rival has set back your company's sales by a mile. You overhear the news: the whole industry has been shaken up by his startup. Surprise, surprise, the company belongs to the *Gordon*

Gekko, and it's *your* corporation that has drunk the poisoned Kool-Aid!

Corporate Gossip: The bread and circuses of the *corporate small fry*. Like the Roman emperors who entertained their *hoi polloi* with gladiators and hungry lions in the Colosseum of ancient Rome, the Boardroom understands the importance of letting corporate gossip run riot to pacify the underclasses by satisfying their bloodlust. They also understand the importance of setting the record straight … if and when *they* want to. Just so soon as any gossip impinges upon corporate performance or threatens to spiral out of the control of top management, especially in times of uncertainty (for the *small fry*), you can count on its being instantly squelched by authoritative emails and voice messages from the top.

Corporate Gotcha: The delighted yelp of the recruitment officer upon receiving the signed offer letter from the fresh, high-calibre, over-motivated graduate from a top law or MBA school, or even from the highly skilled apprentice having just finished his three-year training programme. These enchanting, dewy-eyed freshers actually believe that if you work hard and gain a bit of experience you will have a secure, life-long career in the corporation. Ha! Gotcha!

Corporate Grinch: He really hates *corporate special events*, and Christmas parties in particular! While his colleagues count the days till the next one, the *corporate Grinch* shows a complete lack of fellow-feeling and resists doing his part to make any social event a success. Having read way too many *devil's dictionaries*, he loves to sabotage the festive mood. Nowadays, his last minute cancellations make the *corporate Grinch* harder to spot: like everyone he is under *corporate pressure* to project a "winning image" at all times (or lose his real job). Excuses like "my dog is pregnant" or "I am too tired to move" are telltale signs that you are dealing with a closet *corporate Grinch*.

Corporate Gotcha

Corporate Guru

Corporate Guru: A person in management (quite possibly the only one in your whole corporation) who has somehow conserved his sense of the ethical intact. He's the one and only person you can go to, to make your confession or to seek "spiritual advice" (*i.e.* how not to "lose it" and go stark raving mad). His *seeking* nature wisely accumulated everything you will ever need to find out about yours and his speciality areas. We could all sit around him in a big circle and chant mantras forever – if only there was a chargecode on which they were billable hours.

- H -

Corporate Headhunter: Unlike the aboriginal peoples who remove the heads of slaughtered enemies and preserve them by drying and shrinking the skulls, *corporate headhunters* are downright terrifying. *Corporate headhunters* only hunt the biggest quarry: they are after senior executives and the big commissions they can get if they place them successfully in new corporate posts. *Corporate headhunters* strike greater fear in the hearts of men than their namesakes by their anthropophagic persistency in persuading a corporation's best staff to quit at short notice and go to work for a competitor. But beware: for them *your* career is not what counts, only the commission your new employer will be paying *them*. Just got another *withheld number* call? It may be them!

Corporate Hero: Spider-Man, Superman, Iron Man, Hulk – these are the good guys whom we know from the comic books and movies of our youth. Too bad they never existed in reality: everybody identifies with them, and you wished more than once in your childhood that you had some of their superhuman qualities. Things aren't much different inside the corporation: once

Corporate Hero

in a great while a corporate employee will perform a feat that may seem superhuman; mostly though, it's a case of top management just thinking they have superpowers to over-achieve sales targets and billable hours. But once the reality of their actual management skills sinks in, they have to downsize all over again.

Corporate Hijacker: A pushy, unethical type who robs other employees (and even the occasional executive), shaking down their valuables in the form of ideas, deliverables, even initiatives and programmes. They then shamelessly claim credit for their ill-gotten gains, snagging the promotions and bonuses due to others. *Corporate hijackers* differ from *eggsuckers* in that they commit their heists in broad daylight. They know top executives will turn a blind eye to unethical behaviour which has no legal consequences. We all know how they work: they attend meetings uninvited, send emails behind your back, dump their own work on you, and invite your boss for a "chat" over coffee. Once your hard work pays off, they will be the first to let your boss know about their great success.

Corporate Hot Desking: Companies often have unused desk space at any given time, caused by people being out on the road, on holiday, or in meetings. Thus, the number of desks, furniture and office space needed is actually much less than staff on the telephone list would imply, and a corporation is nothing if not a flinty-eyed cost-cutting machine. Here is the proof Charles Darwin looked for in vain all his life: the survival of him who "gets to the hot desks the firstest with the mostest". But beware: if you're a consultant or salesman, the same *hot desk* too frequently taken becomes a "hot seat". You are not employed to warm chairs; your job is to be on the road, flushing out clients and hunting big bucks for the corporation!

Corporate Hijacker

Corporate HR: This is an "acronym": a word made up of the first letters of the real words in an unwieldy phrase, like NATO for North Atlantic Treaty Organization. In the case of HR the letters stand for *Turkey Farm*. This is the department of every corporation where the "technically challenged" people get dumped along with the politically correct quota hires. HR personnel are the kind who paint by the numbers, never venture any plans or concepts of their own, always play it safe and let borderline decisions be made by others. It's not their fault; they are just not cut out for a corporate world of Machiavellian intrigue and mercurial morals. When times get tough, HR *small fry* are always the first to be flipped out of the frying pan into the fire. Nowadays, *corporate HR* has devolved into a mere "admin" function, leaving the surviving *fry* with nothing to work on but internal presentations, formulas for annual appraisals, diversity recruitment of differently sized, shaped and coloured employees, and other *gobbledy-gobble*. What more evidence is needed that HR looks and sounds most like a turkey farm and its supply chain?

Corporate Human Cubical: This is strictly a nonesuch and a contradiction in terms. Any corporations rumoured to have attempted the development of this impossible project will have failed by now. The very notion is too visionary to be concretely imaginable. It would be easier to send men to the end of the universe than to grasp what a Human Cubical might be. After decades of *corporate meetings*, *corporate telephone conferences* complete with workshops and think-tank symposia, every "People First" corporation on the planet, the authors of this *Dictionary*, and the Devil himself, have all given up on the whole idea.

- 1 -

Corporate Insider: As scientist, philosopher and statesman Francis Bacon had discovered by 1597, "Knowledge is Power". *Corporate insiders* do indeed have "deep" knowledge, but this does not stop with access to confidential information or a corporate reptile's grasp of *corporate politics*. More importantly, they are accepted members of a closed *inner circle* who decide the rise and fall of whole *corporate entities* and their zillions of *small fry*. If you still wonder why it took you 20 hours overtime a week for several years to land that promotion, but the *corporate insider* just one breakfast meeting to land a bonus double the size, then here's a window into their thinking. They care far more for the *ordinal* than the cardinal magnitude of corporate profit: Who shall be *first*, then *second*, then *third* in queue to cut his own slice out of the profit pie? You won't get far *inside* the corporate world with-out thinking this way. ⁱ

- K -

Corporate Kidnapping: An act very similar to *corporate ambush*, but with a more hostile and long-term plan in mind. In this situation, the kidnapper absorbs the victim's previous job role and takes over his entire manpower without his consent. The victim may have already been made obsolete through the introduction of a new management system. To the corporation this makes the victim highly dispensable. But the kidnappee may also be bound over to his new owners through simple negotiation with his seniors, who arrange to have him seconded indefinitely to the kidnapper's own department. By this point no one who understands corporate politics will waste any ransom on such a goner.

Corporate "Kiasu" (a.k.a. "Scared to come last") "Keeping up with the Joneses" is a ubiquitous social anxiety in the modern world, and it's found inside corporations same as elsewhere. Every corporate employee knows at least one *corporate "kiasu"* who preens himself on being always above the pack. He loves comparing himself to you as long as he's actually ahead (and doesn't scruple if he had a head-start). Yet deep down he is threatened by any sign of being shown up by co-workers who are just doing their job. Out peeks the Green-Eyed Monster Envy, playing any trick that will vindicate his self-image – even if that means subverting the whole corporation's interests just to undermine *your* efforts.

- L -

Corporate Labyrinth: The Greek myth tells us that in the dark heart of the original Labyrinth there lurked a Minotaur who every year ate the flesh of young boys and girls. Nowadays it's not so very different: every year fresh graduates are lured after finishing their education to enter the *corporate labyrinth* with no clue (or clew – like the one Ariadne gave Theseus). They end up either being eaten alive or morphing into Minotaurs themselves.

Corporate Leaving Do: This is where you bid a fond farewell to a fellow employee whom you wish had left long ago. Chances are, he is the only one who is sad: – he will miss your entertainment value (see *corporate geek*), or maybe you had been doing his work for him (see *corporate slave*). The conversation at the "do" is at best mundane, not least due to the corporate binge drinking and the ambient roar of drunk people mindlessly chattering. You grinned and pumped their hand at the lunch party organised in their name; now you give rein to fake pathos at the ever embarrassing leaving presentation. You hope you faked it well enough; the fact is, you can scarcely hide your happiness!

Corporate Leaving Do

Corporate Luxury Escort

Corporate Luxury Escort: An employee – usually a *corporate bombshell* or *corporate bird,* or a *corporate Casanova* (if escorting a female) – who accompanies a senior employee to a location, client or formal *corporate special event* such as a ball, cotillion or piss-party, in order to provide protection, support or just company – "normally" in a non-sexual way. (But what actually goes on is anyone's guess ...)

- M -

Corporate Mad Cow: Something the essence of which is hard to put in words; you have to experience it to fully depreciate it. You hear a *corporate mad cow* from the moment you set foot in the office, "Have you updated the report?" Fifteen minutes later she's all over you again, "Have you called the client?" You ask yourself, what have you been doing for the last 80 hours this week? Two hours daydreaming about another job and the rest putting the mad cow out to pasture. Your reverie is brusquely interrupted by the familiar voice – a cow's "moo" would have been more welcome!

Corporate Meetings: This is the place where we all meet for meeting's sake. We are not sure what exactly is achieved, what our objectives are, or what the agenda is, but let's meet anyway. During the endless hours spent in the bored room ... er, boardroom, we never do figure out what's going on, but we console ourselves: at least we got some free hot coffee and crunchy cookies.

Corporate Mentor: Your advocate and your guide through the minefield of *corporate reality*. The *corporate mentor*'s responsibility is to provide advice, sponsorship and encouragement, in good times and bad. Even if all others were to point thumbs down, he is supposed to be the last person to give up on you. In reality he reports all your moves back to upper management, and they all have a good laugh over your false steps, struggles and naivety compared with themselves.

Corporate Miser: The stationery cupboard is empty *again*? The washrooms too are out of toilet paper? The *corporate miser* strikes again! His children need pens and scribbling pads for school; his whole family's hygiene relies on corporate toilet paper. No, the *miser* is not broke, he just can't help being his miserable, penny-pinching, soul-cramped self. You had better keep a sharp eye out for your paper clips and hunker down over your stapler reloads – here he comes again!

Corporate Mole: Like his counterpart in the animal kingdom – that small burrowing mammal that's such a nuisance to farmers and gardeners – the *corporate mole* is a big nuisance to corporate management. His bigmouth braggadocio undermines the corporation in all sorts of subterranean ways. For example, if working on a confidential project, he freely blabs trade secrets and corporate intelligence to his friends on the outside. The word spreads and invisibly disrupts corporate harmony and saps morale and team spirit, wreaking both tangible and intangible damage. He may even pass confidential information on to *corporate competitors*, following the example of his namesake in the world of espionage. Have you noticed anyone lately who is quite talkative yet regards you with a certain degree of suspicion? He might be the one.

Corporate Mole Catcher: This scalp-hunting type may be found in Audit, Internal Controls, Compliance or Quality Risk Management departments. They suspect *corporate moles* everywhere and see their destructive powers as a risk, not as a challenge. *Mole catchers* get appraised on the number of "velvety furs" successfully *skinned*.

Corporate Mushroom: Like fungi on the forest floor *corporate mushrooms* live in the shadows. They are most often found hiding behind their computer screens, where no clients can harm them. Careful! If by sheer accident you trip over one, wounding their delicate tissue and breaking off a bit of their self-esteem, they may need the rest of their office life to recover confidence. Offenders who bruise their delicate tissues may end up blind (or blindsided) by an unforeseen dose of toxicity, like an atrociously misspelled letter to an important client, or a miskept appointment diary.

- N -

Corporate Neglect: A situation where a *negligor* is neglecting a *negligee* who is "desperately seeking" *corporate brownie points* by pandering to the negligor. The negligor closes his "always open" door by filtering his calls and sends the negligee's straight to voicemail, or making his diary for private view only. Cases of *corporate neglect* easily escalate to outright *corporate abuse*. Some negligees will sell themselves into *corporate slavery* to try and roll back *neglect*. As usual, *corporate HR* deny to the death that *corporate neglect* exists: they and management are "always open" to People First Firm, but *corporate neglect* is a fact of life inside the beast, and is in fact becoming more widespread.

Corporate Nerd: He may look like Bill Gates, but without the big money backing him up. He is the expert we all consult when we need technical advice, but at other times we might walk over his face by accident. He'd probably do better to make like Steve Jobs and start all over from his parents' garage.

Corporate Nerd

Corporate Never-Never Land: The "Never-Never" can refer to Peter Pan's fairy-tale world of eternal youth, or the harshest, remotest parts of the Australian Outback. *Corporate Never-Never Land* seems glorious like the first, but in reality is dismal like the last.

Your own Never-Never is a fishbowl which everybody can see through except you. The irony is, they who see through yours can't see through their own. Thus, thousands of employees high and low live in their own fishbowl dreamworlds, believing they are the best performing "breed" in the cubical on their level, doing a job no one else can do. Welcome to *corporate Never-Never Land!*

Corporate Nightmare: This always happens when you least expect it. It differs from Murphy's Law ("If it can go wrong, it will") only in adding the codicil "… and everything that will go wrong, will do so at the same time". Remember that PA you fired at your last job? In your new job she has become your boss, and you are demoted to the stationery department to hand out paper clips. Since you can't wake up out of this *corporate nightmare*, you are forced to confront your own fallibility. You find all your dreams and aspirations sinking into the floor. It's time to sink or swim!

- O -

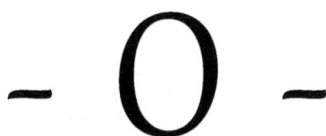

Corporate Outlaw: Corporations are often described in terms resembling the Wild West; for example, in a corporation with a strong sales force the salesmen are called *cowboys*. In a similar vein, *corporate outlaws*, whether jumping intellectual property claims or rustling human cattle, are clearly operating "outside" corporate "law". Trade secrets, customers, marketing ideas and in general everything that bids fair to make big money has been "branded" like a cow with the owner's logo and is to be kept inside the corporation that branded it. A *corporate outlaw* caught in the act will be named and shamed, then unceremoniously sacked and blacklisted – the corporate equivalent of hanging 'em from the highest tree.

Corporate Outsourcing: Like the laying hens in "battery-farms" that produce eggs for bargain-hunting consumers, outsourcing providers employ "redundant" *corporate small fry* to offer cheapened services for cost reduction-hungry corporations and their shareholders. Outsourcing saves money in the short term, but

Corporate Outlaw

eventually it undermines working moral and drains knowledge from the corporation. The moral of the story: When the fox is guarding the henhouse, better fly the coop before you're next on the menu!

Corporate Overtime: You think you're going to work some extra hours and supplement your income or make up time lost in meetings. Ha! No such luck. You're on salary, mate. That means the corporation can require you to work any number of hours for nothing more than the fixed amount you agreed in the beginning. Welcome to a lifetime of *corporate slavery*!

- P -

Corporate Paradise: A Fool's Paradise by definition. A thoroughly devilish *frisson* of ecstasy as a result of events that convince the fool that he lords it over lesser (or in his mind greater) fools. It may be something as petty as reading a memo that praises your work. In theory it may be savoured by anyone, but *corporate slaves* (for example) rarely adventure into paradise. And when once in a blue moon lightning does strike (like in the Smurfs' mushroom land), paradise for these sad sacks never lasts. For senior management of course, everything is different: the highest ranking corporate officers spend their whole lives in the corporation's artificial paradise, being fawned over by hundreds of *corporate slaves*.

Corporate Pension: What employees look forward to after 40 years or more of endless drudgery working for a *grateful corporation*. Not unlike the Irish farmer chasing the end of the rainbow looking for that legendary Pot o' Gold, the corporate pension can prove an elusive creature. If your corporation goes bankrupt or

Corporate Pensions

is taken over in a merger or acquisition, you can colour your pension "gone". Don't bother suing for recovery. You have about as much chance of collecting what you're owed as of catching a Leprechaun!

Corporate Pipsqueak (a.k.a. Junior Officer): The corporate share price is in free fall and top management hold an emergency meeting to brainstorm innovative ideas for turning the corporation around, bringing in a guaranteed return on investment. *Pipsqueak* pipes up:

"I have a great idea! Let's close down our investment bank and reincorporate as a mental hospital. That would suit us better anyway, and the public will believe we've finally seen the light and are seeking help. In hard times like this, we have plenty of broken (but not yet broke) former clients and customers who will gladly join us at our newly opened funny farm. Since we will be unemployed, our wives will have to work. We can hire them as psychiatric nurses: then they will have to pamper *us* while we nag *them*". Pipsqueak's stroke of genius is greeted with an embarrassed silence.

The moral of the story? The world's best ideas fall to the *pipsqueaks*, while those with all the power to change the world love it "as is".

Corporate Pittance: Try living on this for a week. It may be enough to feed your dog or cat. If there are any crumbs left, you can suck them up with your lips. As they say, anything is better than nothing!

Corporate Politics: The most intangible asset a corporation has on its books – a bit like liabilities and owners' equity. *Corporate fatcats* seem to have been born knowing how to play the games that will boost their status or power within organisations. By contrast *corporate small fry* are naïve fledgelings in the gladiators' arena of *corporate politics*. Middle management fall somewhere in the middle of the corporate playground: allowed to build little sandcastles ... which are instantly pulverised by the *fatcats* should they ever challenge the essential *status quo*. Yet even masters of *corporate politics* are not invulnerable. For them intrigues and manoeuvres to gain power and influence are the daily bread, and the boardroom may be the bloodiest psycho-chamber in the whole organisation.

Corporate Pressure: An invisible force acting at a distance and transcendent as to time and place. In some quarters it is rumoured to be the force that began the universe. Nowadays it causes employees to manage their time to the minute; try to please unforgiving managers; and pore over their work to *exact* it to uncompromising specifications. As in the ocean, so also in the corporate hierarchy: the lower down the *career ladder* you descend, the more overbearing the pressure. But *corporate pressure* may also be self-inflicted: employees feel themselves constantly under pressures that don't actually exist ... at least not yet!

Corporate Prisoner: A worker chained to his job like a galley slave, unable to leave for various possible reasons. It could be because of a recessionary labour market, insufficient skills to take the next step up the career ladder, or simply a lack of trust to reach out to headhunters and friends who might help. It could even be unpaid debts. There is a view that *corporate prisoners* are bad for business and undermine morale: if they become desperate to escape but can't, they disengage from the corporation and may turn into *corporate renegades* or, in the worst case, *corporate outlaws*.

Corporate Profile: This is the photo of you and employee number kept by HR. However, if you behave in any way that annoys someone with just a little bit more administrative power than you, it can be used against you like a Wild West "Wanted" poster. It then becomes your corporate mug-shot.

Corporate Profits: An annoying accountancy detail of no interest to top management, so long as it is fat enough to subsidise their salaries, perks and bonuses.

Corporate Prisoner

- R -

Corporate Reality: Accessed *via* the employee entrance, over which hangs the infernal sentence: "Abandon all hope ye who enter these gates". Please note: to inform corporate readers about *corporate reality* would mean waking them up out of their *corporate dreaming*, which could lead to terminal *corporate blues*. We have been advised that this should never happen without medical assistance at hand. Please make an appointment with your in-house witch-doctor or impersonal shrink (see *corporate HR*) to learn more about *corporate reality*. As T. S. Eliot famously penned, "Mankind cannot bear very much reality".

Corporate Recorded Message: You phone in to your office to run something by a fellow employee, and the recorded message chirps: "I am not at my desk at the moment, but will return your call when I get back". You smile knowingly, recognising that as corporate lingo for "I'm chained to my desk like a galley slave but somehow managed to wangle a 5-minute toilet break from the boss".

Corporate References: These are the folk you have shamelessly sucked up to in hopes of "advancing your career" at a later date. When you finally get downsized instead (which nowadays doesn't take long), you whine and wag your puppy-dog tail as you beg and wheedle "letters of reference" to show prospective employers, which supposedly attest that it wasn't because of incompetence that you got the sack (probably?).

Corporate Renegade: Unlike the *corporate outlaw*, the *corporate renegade* has not (yet) profaned the corporation's sacred cows ... er, standards of appropriate conduct – and for that matter will never disregard universal ethical norms. He may ignore elements of corporate policy, abstain from the usual dodgy shortcuts, and forswear blind allegiance to "senior management"; but his own decency forbids him to betray his brothers and sisters inside the corporation. He is just a *renegade*. Beware: if kept too long in isolation, disgruntled and without eulogy, he might turn into a whistle-blower or *outlaw*.

Corporate Reorganisation: Like deer caught spellbound in the headlamps of an oncoming lorry and run over, *corporate small fry* are hypnotised by the magic word "reorganisation". It promises a new beginning and better life, so why would anyone suspect an apocalypse?

In reality, *reorganisation* is a label-switch for "redundancy" used to forestall turmoil in the workforce: it misleads them about what to expect. It is how the *corporate fat cats* justify themselves: they hide their own blunders by reorganizing the corporation every six months in the name of "savings and efficiency".

Corporate Reptile: Because the "entity" is competing for profits with many other entities in an environment of "un-natural" selection, there is pressure on top management to see to the *survival of the fittest* salaries, perks and bonuses. Thus, those with the scaliest skin and most primitive survival instincts will succeed. These *corporate reptiles* love to put "selection pressure" on

Corporate Reptile

their next-in-line ("Others can be *selected* to replace you"). This pressure is *by nature* passed down the *food chain* until the whole "entity" from top to bottom is completely controlled by it (see also *corporate pressure*).

Corporate Retard: It used to be that every organisation had one. Nowadays one is not enough – there has to be one in every department (at the least). Of course he's slow and retards your performance, but what's worse is that *you* seem to attract so many of them. The retard in *corporate HR* will not respond to queries – "everything is online now", even if the amount of time needed to find it is an order of magnitude longer than if he would just answer the question. The retard from IT support offers to fix your laptop problems at your office desk, but only while you're on client site where you need it the most. As you enter the conference room for you weekly team telco, you notice *another* retard who was there before you has taken the conference phone with him. How the corporate balance sheet survives all the retards is one of life's little mysteries.

- S -

Corporate Sabotage: An act performed only by employees of the *corporate entity*, nearly always a trade-off for *corporate blues*. If depression does not dominate their thoughts, they will have turned to the destruction of corporate value. Disillusioned with *corporate reality*, saboteurs no longer feel concern about the future, their present life, or the "parent entity". The impulse to *corporate sabotage* may even pursue senior employees. If it catches up, beware the *corporate dynamite*!

Corporate Sadist: Like the Marquis de Sade, who tortured and poisoned prostitutes, then spent 30 years of his life in an insane asylum, the *corporate Sadist*, typically a member of senior management, is one who enjoys bringing *corporate blues* down upon subaltern staff through cunningly camouflaged forms of *corporate abuse*. As the *corporate Sadist* watches his victims squirm, his tail grows longer than the Devil's.

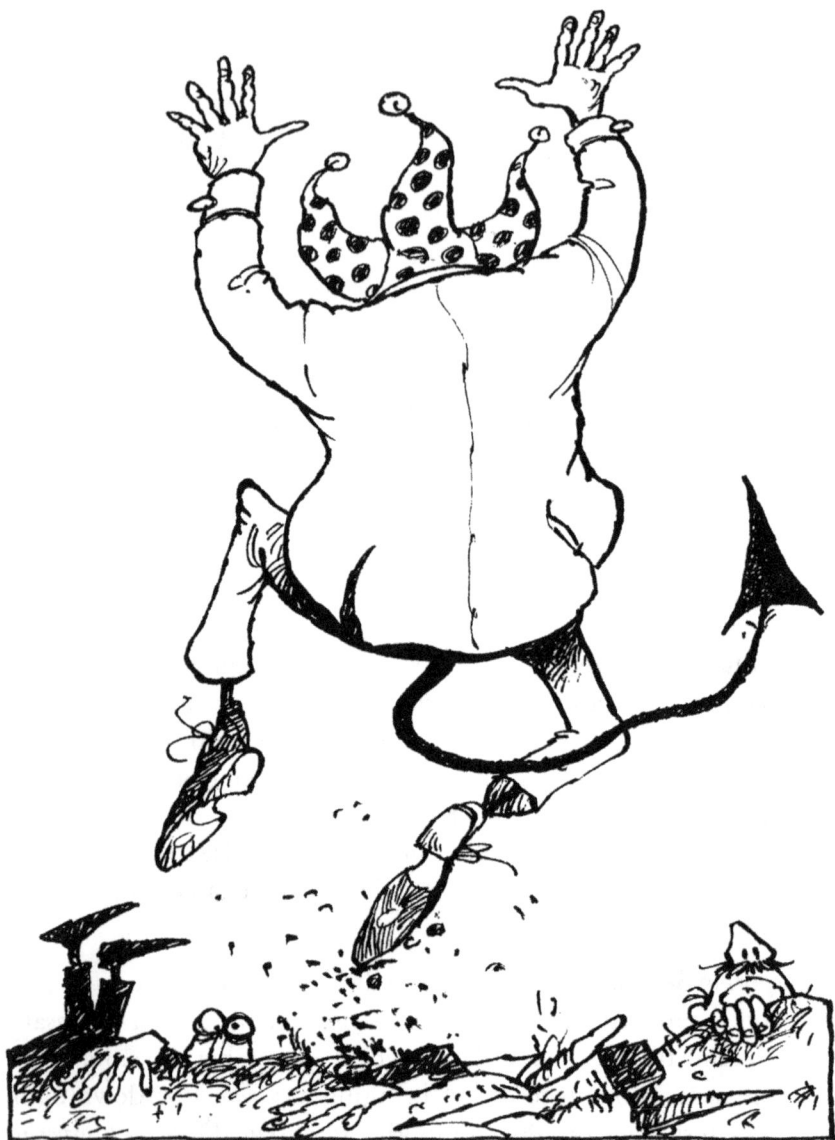

Corporate Sadist

Corporate Scaredy-Cat: One who is afraid of everything: his colleagues, his boss, the daily routine, corporate life. This kind of fear is what the higher-ups love to see: it makes of an employee a loyal *corporate slave* who will never speak up unless asked. They don't foresee that *scaredy-cat* will eventually have to take a long "stress leave" when he can't cope anymore.

Corporate Scrooge: Like Ebenezer in Dickens's *A Christmas Carol*, the grump who is the corporate top boss spends the least money. He celebrates the financial success of his organisation without spending anything on food or drink. Or he invites his team to Christmas dinner, but expects them to pay for themselves ("I pay them a salary, don't I?"). One day, the Ghost of Christmas Bonuses Past may visit him in his guilty dreams and replay all the wrongdoings of his corporate life, converting him into a more pleasant character. (But don't hold your breath waiting ... !)

Corporate Self-Destruct Button: Otherwise known by the genteel expression "TAKE THIS JOB AND SHOVE IT!!" You might consider using it when your career has dead-ended, or simply because nobody in the office seems to care any more whether you exist. To be used in an emergency only and at your own risk!

Corporate Sheriff: The officer in the corporation who enforces *law and order* and compliance with company policies. Instead of hanging *corporate outlaws* and *corporate renegades*, however, *corporate sheriffs* serve them warning letters and other career-melting stigmata. *Corporate sheriffs* are found in legal and internal audit as well as in compliance departments. Although shoot-outs are rare these days, *corporate sheriffs* often "trigger" the *corporate blues*.

Corporate Show: Often initiated by senior management with the objective of attracting attention and ultimately making financial gains. It's like with Hollywood blockbusters: just as the entertainment industry wants hordes of people to queue up at the box office, so senior management love it when their corporate shows are followed by employees (as well as clients, suppliers and the media).

Corporate Siesta: In Mexico, many Mediterranean countries, and others near the equator it is a common practice for white-collar employees to take an afternoon nap from 1 to 3pm. In chillier countries that take a dim view of the warm south, a siesta during "working hours" can prompt a disciplinary warning letter. But *corporate slaves* and *small fry* are pesky little varmints; soon enough they had found a workaround – replacing *siestas* with *coffee catch-ups*. It helps us through that most difficult time of the day. All you need do is fake like you're still awake.

Corporate Slave: The social and legal designation of workers as bound by chains visible or invisible to their owner (in our latter days *a.k.a.* "employer" or "corporation") and obliged to provide labour and services. *Corporate slaves* might as well be property, since they are treated like it. Their formal rights don't spare them the iron necessity of working themselves to the bone. They are without the right either to refuse work, or to gain (appropriate) compensation (see *corporate pittance*). *Corporate slaves* are complete dependents upon the corporation. Indeed, long-term *corporate slaves* in particular may not recognize their slave status anymore. Yet their employer provides them with literally everything: a salary to pay the mortgage; their tech gizmos (barely having the wherewithal for a private Blackberry, mobile phone, laptop etc.); even their leisure plans, as their lives must be structured around appraisals, annual development plans, *etc.* – thus, even their "shopping" and "social life" may be organised by the corporation. The brighter ones can dream of one day being freed by a Spartacus. (But we know how *that* story turned out ...)

Corporate Small Fry: Most corporate employees are like "fry" or plankton in the ocean. The big fish eat them by the thousands without even noticing their meal consists of individuals ... and still they are hungry for more. If you fancy yourself a valued or an *important* employee, better think twice. Your notice of dismissal could already be in the post!

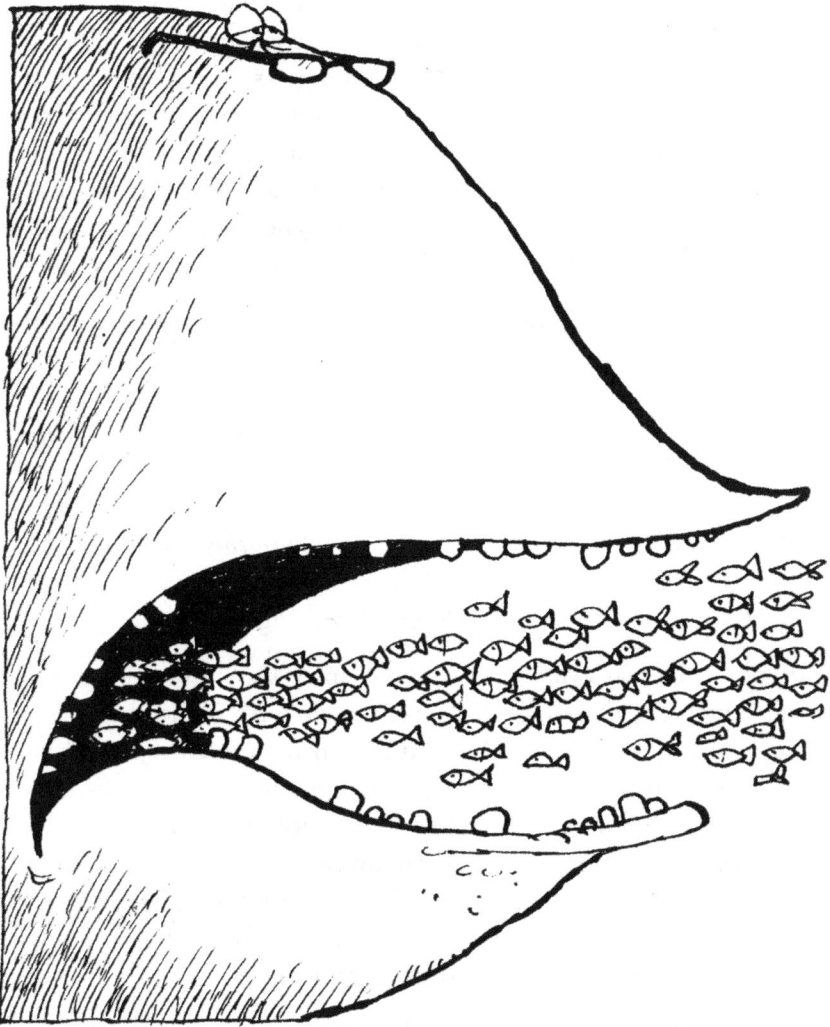

Corporate Small Fry

Corporate Social Responsibility Day: When you're supposed to "give back to the community". That it's only one day out of the year says it all. On this one day the corporation puts its "social responsibility" on display by forcing voluntary labour on its *slaves* and *small fry*. In their trainers and washed-out jeans they have to paint walls, build fences with barbed wire, plant cactus, move haystacks, feed donkeys and pigs, and last but not least fill little blue plastic bags with dung. The underlings go along with these delights like dead fish float in the stream.

Corporate Spam : Corporations generate spam-like volumes of internal emails to thousands of people who – already straining to keep up with the emails that really matter – will never, ever read them; but which *impacts* (as in "lunar *impact* crater") local IT network performance as well as your capacity to perform your daily work. Worse still is when you get invited to their mandatory "communications update meetings", where *they* tell *you* how to work more effectively. Is that clear? Most annoying is that you can't unsubscribe from the internal mailing list.

Corporate Special Event: An extravagantly showy social function at which the corporation's big shots vie with each other to run up the highest bill in celebrating their own celebrity. Like the proverbial valet in whose eyes no man is a hero, *corporate small fry* and other low-level employees are suitably unimpressed. They let the higher-ups get on with immortalizing their corporate lives with their triumphal *special event*, whilst they, having given up on having a life, attend only to guzzle fruity designer wine enough to obliterate their own insignificance.

Corporate Strategy: The official "blueprint" that informs all employees which direction the corporation will pursue in the future and by what means. The plan is so supremely important it's at least 10 years out of date, and so deeply meaningful that nobody remembered to update it.

Corporate Stock Pension: (see also *Corporate Pension*) Also known as the "pension [piss] pot", low-level employees seldom understand how piss-poor and underfunded their own pot is. Typically, the *corporate fat cats* who sucked the value out of the corporation have long since bailed out in their Golden Parachutes. As a result *corporate small fry* get to take a Golden Shower. Endowment pensions from an insolvent insurance scheme or stock and shares pensions are prone to becoming worthless or nearly so – thanks precisely to corporate mismanagement of insurance companies. No worries, mate; pensions follow the natural business cycle. If you end up with nothing, you can console yourself with the thought of the many lessons you have learned from your life now that it's over. Why, for one thing you've learned it's better to rely on bonuses than pensions. Wow, what a lesson! You can bank that one on your way to *Doomsday* ...

Corporate Surfer: The employee who is always "connected" and "networking" *via* the Internet, his iPhone, his Blackberry, Twitter, Facebook, LinkedIn and God Knows Whatnot. Powered by Jawbone, he lives on Canteen Coffee. This species is a pep-talker, but you begin to wonder if everything really can be going that relentlessly well day after day after day. Don't be surprised if by next week he has surfed on to the next corporate shore.

Corporate Synergy: A word that we learned during our last Greek island-hopping holiday: συνεργεια. It means "working together", but in such a way that the whole effort is greater than the sum of its parts. Less well known is how the concept synergises with its own context. In a commercial context it means that businesses which reduce costs and boost revenues by providing complementary services and processes incidentally gain control over their own supply chain. In a consultancy context it simply means (hacking through the hokum) that "two heads are better than one". In still other contexts it may be harder to define. Rumour has it that certain corporate personnel who are *undoubtedly* everybody's favourite folks – legal counsel, internal auditors, quality controllers, risk and compliance officers – synergise best with Davy Jones's locker (you know ... the one at the bottom of the sea?) ... but this is only a rumour ...

CORPORATE SURFER

- T -

Corporate Team Building Day: Rome wasn't built in a day and neither is *corporate teamwork*. This is one day you could have done without. It feels like being in the army, with all the physical exercises you have to huff and puff through, wearing boots and helmet (as required for "health and safety"). The best parts, however, are the exercises where your shadiest colleagues have to depend on you and your mates – the one who delegated the impossible tasks, the other one who made you lose out on that promotion, or that one over there who ambushed you into working all those late hours. Oops! While you were hoisting him fifteen feet in the air with a forklift to pick apples off the tree he "had an accident". *Corporate teamwork* strikes again.

Corporate Teamwork: The Oxford English Dictionary defines teamwork as "the combined action of a group, especially when effective and efficient". *Corporate teamwork* is indeed a combined action, but there ends any resemblance to what dreaming dons suppose teamwork to be. Ostensibly, the team's competitive

Corporate Teamwork

instincts strive outward after every corporation's goals of profit-maximisation and market domination. In reality, it is probably the main arena of infighting inside corporate walls. The evidence that *corporate teamwork* causes internal casualties is undeniable and seen everywhere in the form of redundancies and sackings, mental illness, alcoholism, and broken homes.

Corporate Telco (or Telephone Conference): A telephone call with more than two parties on the line. This does not necessarily mean that more than two parties are actually listening to the conversation. Normally, a secret PIN coder is distributed to the participants, which activates the "conference bridge". Junior staff with little experience of what *corporate telcos* are for, are elated at being invited to join the charmed circle of senior colleagues! They soon find out they're just errand boys – there to take the minutes – or worse, poor devils to be stuck with responsibility to meet the impossible deadlines agreed. To minimise background noise (railway stations, airports, crying babies, the snoring of senior partners), you are asked to keep your telephone on "mute" until it's your turn to chime in. Crestfallen newbies, however, are ordered to mute their telephones for the duration. As stern Victorian parents used to say, "Children are to be seen and not heard!"

Corporate Time Sheet: If you work in professional services, you know this as the volatile ingredient that can get you sacked quicker than anything, even murder or demanding a pay rise. One missed time sheet and your counsellor will be notified. Two missed and the head of your department will have a "serious word" (*viz.* an ominous threat) with you. Three and the axe-wielding executioner from HR is demanding your head ... er, serving you your first formal warning. What did you do to deserve the chopping block? Why, you missed the deadline for submitting your almighty chargeable hours, mate – the stuff of the CEO's eight-figure salary and far more valuable than any time spent on training, admin and other no-account virtues.

Corporate Telco

- V -

Corporate Value: Value is generally defined as "an amount of money considered to be a fair exchange for something". Corporations consider customers, stakeholders and *their* services of high value. But never overestimate your *corporate value*. Your last salary increase was a clear indication of *your* value for the corporation.

- W -

Corporate Witch: Ever thought that if you were quick enough, you might glimpse a female colleague flying about the office on a broomstick? Then you may be sharing your office with a *corporate witch*. The hardest to spot are the dulcet-voiced ones, who seem to practice sorcery on their male colleagues: "Can you fetch that file from the stationery room, dear? Can you help me to finish this presentation? Can you cover me in the client presentation?" If your response to any of these requests is resentment yet submissiveness out of fear of offending her, better double-check your *cojones*, brother. Maybe you're bewitched already!

Corporate World Traveller: After years of saving up, the *corporate world traveller* is finally about to fulfil his American Dream Trip. Excited about his plans and eager to go, he approaches workmates who've been there and done that. For how many years have they overheard him bragging about all the countries he has visited? They always did wonder how he managed it in the little holiday time left available to him by the demands of his bosses.

Corporate Witch

But of course! – he tuned into World Discovery Channel every night and in the daytime he surfed Google Street Maps … but *never* on company time!

Corporate Worshipper: He worships his corporation and its brand name like a demi-god. His love and devotion to his corporation is endless. Never irreverence the entity in which he plays a leading role, or you may find your friendship with him in ruins. He celebrates *corporate special events* as sacred rites, and sacrifices his and others' blood for the corporation's success. Rising profits and competitive supremacy isn't everything, it's the only thing. Where does it end, this intense love and admiration for himself in the image of his corporation? Maybe when he is forced to take early retirement and his access to his office is disabled. Maybe not even then …

Corporate Wuss: Let's face it, we are surrounded by *corporate wussies* at all times. Not speaking up in the meeting, although one has valuable information that might bring about a salutary revision of a failing project; apathetically following the latest sales initiative, knowing full well the market won't buy it; going along with a new technology that has flaws one is aware of; all these are signs of wussiness. For *small fry*, however, it is a rarefied metaphysical line that divides being a wuss from knowing your place. Sometimes it makes us wonder if *corporate wussies* aren't simply the Jedi masters of the corporate game.

- Z -

Corporate Zombie: The undead of the corporate world, the *corporate zombie* makes a frightful appearance. The long hours spent staring at computer screens while sitting in anti-ergonomic office chairs causes the hunchbacked posture and the dark rings under the eyes. Too much to drink at last night's *leaving do* causes that splitting headache and that ringing in the ears that drives the walking corpse into erratic behaviour mode. If only they were feeding on their bosses' flesh instead of their own ...

Corporate Zombie